THESE PRAYERS AND PROMISES ARE LIFTED UP IN FAITH BY:

_____

FOR THE PRECIOUS BODY, SOUL, AND SPIRIT OF:

_____

Pour out your heart like water before the face of the Lord.
Lift your hands toward Him
for the life of your young children.

LAMENTATIONS 2:19

Prayers *and* Promises *for* My Little Boy

Stormie Omartian

Artwork by TOM BROWNING

HARVEST HOUSE PUBLISHERS

EUGENE, OREGON

PRAYERS AND PROMISES FOR MY LITTLE BOY

Text copyright © 2008 by Stormie Omartian
Artwork copyright © 2008 by Tom Browning
Published by Harvest House Publishers
Eugene, Oregon 97402
www.harvesthousepublishers.com

ISBN-13: 978-0-7369-2159-6
ISBN-10: 0-7369-2159-1

Please visit Tom Browning's website at www.tombrowning.com

Prayers adapted from content featured in

The Power of a Praying® Parent Book of Prayers
Copyright © 2004 by Stormie Omartian
Published by Harvest House Publishers

The Power of a Praying® Parent
Copyright © 1995 by Stormie Omartian
Published by Harvest House Publishers

Production and design by Koechel Peterson & Associates, Inc., Minneapolis, Minnesota

Unless otherwise indicated, Scripture quotations are taken from the New King James Version. Copyright ©1982 by Thomas Nelson, Inc. Used by permission. All rights reserved. Verses marked NIV are taken from the HOLY BIBLE, NEW INTERNATIONAL VERSION®. NIV®. Copyright©1973, 1978, 1984 by the International Bible Society. Used by permission of Zondervan. All rights reserved.

Printed in China

09 10 11 12 13 14 15 16 / IM / 10 9 8 7 6 5 4

CONTENTS

Behold, children are a heritage from the LORD,
the fruit of the womb is a reward.

PSALM 127:3

Prayer of Gratitude
for My Little Boy

LORD, THANK YOU for my little boy. He is such a wonderful gift to me. Help me to raise him well. May the beauty of Your Spirit be so evident in me that I will be a godly role model for him. Give me the communication, teaching, and nurturing skills that I must have. Grow me into being the kind of parent You want me to be and teach me how to pray and truly intercede for his life.

I'm grateful that I don't have to rely on the world's unreliable and ever-changing methods of child rearing, but that I can have clear directions from Your Word and wisdom as I pray to You for guidance. I rely on You for everything, and this day I trust my child to You and release him into Your hands.

In Jesus' name I ask that You will increase my faith for all the things You have put on my heart to pray for concerning my son.

BELIEVING IN GOD'S PROMISES FOR HIM

I will pour water on him who is thirsty,
and floods on the dry ground;
I will pour My Spirit on your descendants,
and My blessing on your offspring.

ISAIAH 44:3

Whatever you ask in My name,
that I will do,
that the Father may be glorified in the Son.
If you ask anything in My name,
I will do it.

JOHN 14:13-14

PRAYER FOR
commitment

Prayer for My Son's Commitment to God

LORD, I PRAY that You would give my son a heart devoted to You and obedient to You. Put into him a longing to spend time with You, in Your Word, and in prayer, listening for Your voice. Shine Your light upon any secret or unseen rebellion that is taking root in his heart, so that it can be revealed and eliminated.

May (child's name) not give himself over to pride, selfishness, and rebellion. I pray that disrespect and idolatry will have no part in my son's character so that all he does and says reflects a life devoted to You.

BELIEVING IN GOD'S PROMISES FOR HIM

If you are willing and obedient,
you shall eat the good of the land.

ISAIAH 1:19

Incline my heart to Your testimonies, and not to covetousness. Turn away my eyes from looking at worthless things, and revive me in Your way. Establish Your word to Your servant, who is devoted to fearing You.

PSALM 119:36-38

Prayer for My Son's Wisdom and Understanding

LORD, I PRAY that You would give the gifts of wisdom, discernment, and revelation to (name of child). Help him not depend on his own understanding, but acknowledge You in all his ways so that he may hear Your clear direction as to which path to take.

I know his happiness depends on gaining wisdom and discernment, which Your Word says brings long life, wealth, recognition, protection, enjoyment, contentment, and happiness. May these come to him because of Your gift of wisdom.

BELIEVING IN GOD'S PROMISES FOR HIM

*We know that the Son of God has come and has given us an understanding,
that we may know Him who is true;
and we are in Him who is true, in His Son Jesus Christ.
This is the true God and eternal life.*

1 JOHN 5:20

understanding

The fear of the LORD
is the beginning of wisdom;
all who follow his precepts
have good understanding.
To him belongs eternal praise.

PSALM 111:10 NIV

Prayer for My Son's Peace and Acceptance

LORD, I PRAY for my son to feel loved and accepted. Penetrate his heart with Your love right now and help him to understand how far-reaching and complete it is. You love us so much that You sent Your Son to die for us. Deliver my boy from anything that causes him to doubt that.

Help him to abide in Your love with peace and certainty. May he say as David did, "Cause me to hear Your loving-kindness in the morning, for in You do I trust" (Psalm 143:8). Manifest Your love to this child in a real way today and help him to receive it.

God is love, and he who abides in love
abides in God, and God in him.

1 JOHN 4:16

All your sons will be taught by the LORD,

and great will be your children's peace.

ISAIAH 54:13 NIV

SPEAK A BLESSING

My wonderful son

My wonderful son, may the Lord grant you understanding in all things.
I pray that your sense of truth and righteousness comes only from His
Word and His grace. May you always have a discerning spirit so that your
every step is guided by God (2 Timothy 2:7).

May the Lord bless you with a measure of faith that is deep, strong,
and unfailing. As I raise you with a solid foundation built on faith in God,
may your own relationship with the Lord always give you the courage
to trust Him no matter what is going on in your life (Romans 12:3).

Prayer for My Son's Safety and Security

THANK YOU, LORD, for Your promises of protection. I pray that You will put a hedge of safety and protection around my son to keep him from harm. May fear never hold him back from trusting the security he has in You. I pray specifically for protection from accidents, disease, injury, or any physical, mental, or emotional trauma.

Help him to walk in Your ways and in obedience to Your will so that he never comes out from under the umbrella of that protection. Keep him safe in all he does and wherever he goes.

BELIEVING IN GOD'S PROMISES FOR HIM

The fear of man brings a snare,
but whoever trusts in the LORD shall be safe.

PROVERBS 29:25

*I will both lie down
in peace,
and sleep;
for You alone, O LORD,
make me dwell in safety.*

PSALM 4:8

PRAYER FOR *confidence*

Prayer for My Son's Confidence in the Lord

LORD, I PRAY that my son will live a fruitful life, ever increasing in the knowledge of You. May he always know Your will, have spiritual understanding, and walk in a manner that is pleasing in Your sight. I pray You would pour out Your Spirit upon my son so that he will comprehend the fullness of Your forgiveness. May he never live in guilt and condemnation but by faith and with confidence.

I pray that my son won't doubt Your love or stray from the path or the work of faith You have for him.

BELIEVING IN GOD'S PROMISES FOR HIM

I will pray the Father, and He will give you another Helper,
that He may abide with you forever—the Spirit of truth,
whom the world cannot receive, because it neither sees Him nor knows Him;
but you know Him, for He dwells with you and will be in you.

JOHN 14:16-17

We also pray always for you that our God would count you
worthy of this calling, and fulfill all the good pleasure of His goodness
and the work of faith with power, that the name of our Lord Jesus Christ
may be glorified in you, and you in Him, according to the grace
of our God and the Lord Jesus Christ.

2 THESSALONIANS 1:11-12

Prayer for My Son's Strong Family Relationships

LORD, I PRAY for (name of child) and his relationship with all family members. Protect and preserve them from any unresolved disputes or troubles. Strengthen them so that they never fail. Fill his heart with Your love so that he always has an abundance of compassion and forgiveness.

I pray for a close, happy, loving, and fulfilling relationship between my son and the rest of the family. May there always be good communication, and may we always love, value, appreciate, and respect one another so that the God-ordained tie between us cannot be broken.

BELIEVING IN GOD'S PROMISES FOR HIM

Behold, how good
and how pleasant it is
for brethren to dwell together in unity!

PSALM 133:1

The righteous man walks
in his integrity;
his children are blessed after him.

PROVERBS 20:7

Blessed are the peacemakers,
for they shall be called sons of God.

MATTHEW 5:9

COMPASSION

Prayer for My Son's Compassion for Others

LORD, I PRAY that You would teach my son to resolve misunderstandings according to Your Word. And if any division has already begun, if any relationship is strained or severed, I pray You will drive out the wedge of division and bring healing.

Please give my son a heart of forgiveness and reconciliation. Help him to live "endeavoring to keep the unity of the Spirit in the bond of peace" (Ephesians 4:3). In Jesus' name I pray that You would instill a strong love and compassion in him for others.

BELIEVING IN GOD'S PROMISES FOR HIM

Be kind to one another, tenderhearted,
forgiving one another,
even as God in Christ forgave you.

EPHESIANS 4:32

A man who has friends must himself be friendly,
but there is a friend who sticks closer than a brother.

PROVERBS 18:24

Praying for My Son's Good, Godly Friendships

LORD, I PRAY that my son will always have good, godly friendships. Help him to be free from anyone in his life who has an ungodly character or will be a bad influence. Take away any loneliness or low self-esteem that would cause him to seek out less than God-glorifying relationships.

Teach him how to be a good friend and make strong, close, lasting relationships. Whenever there is grief over a lost friendship, comfort him and send new friends with whom he can connect, share, and be the person You created him to be. I pray You would help him to understand the meaning of true friendship.

BELIEVING IN GOD'S PROMISES FOR HIM

If they fall, one will lift up his companion.
But woe to him who is alone when he falls,
for he has no one to help him up.

ECCLESIASTES 4:10

Blessings

SPEAK A BLESSING

My son, as you learn about life, as you train in school, as you explore
your surroundings, and as you examine your faith,
may you grow in reverence for God and in understanding
of His power and mercy. May you see at an early age
that only He can bring you true wisdom and understanding.
Let His light lead you in your quest for answers and meaning (Proverbs 9:10).

May you always sense God's love in your life.
As deep as my love is for you, the Lord's love is even greater.
He always loves you no matter what,
and He wants you to love Him in that same way.
When you do, He will give you the ability to love others without condition,
without demands, and without criticism.
May you always seek to be close to God and enjoy the fullness
and depth of the love He has for you (1 John 4:10-11).

Prayer for My Son's Ability to Lead

LORD, I PRAY that You would pour out Your Spirit upon my son this day and anoint him for all that You've called him to be and do. May he never stray from Your path and try to be something he was not created to be.

May he not be a follower of anyone but You, but may he become a leader who has a godly, noble character. Specifically, I pray he will lead people into Your kingdom. May the fruit of the Spirit—love, joy, peace, patience, kindness, goodness, faithfulness, gentleness, and self-control—grow in him daily (Galatians 5:22-23 NIV).

BELIEVING IN GOD'S PROMISES FOR HIM

Be even more diligent to make your call and election sure,
for if you do these things you will never stumble.

2 PETER 1:10

leadership

Eye has not seen, nor ear heard,
nor have entered into the heart of man
the things which God has prepared
for those who love Him.

1 CORINTHIANS 2:9

Prayer for My Son's Health and Healing

LORD, BECAUSE YOU have instructed us in Your Word that we are to pray for one another so that we may be healed, I pray for healing and wholeness for (name of child). I pray that sickness and infirmity will have no place in his life.

I pray for protection against any disease coming into his body. Whenever there is disease, illness, or weakness in him, I pray that You, Lord, would touch him with Your healing power and restore him to total health.

BELIEVING IN GOD'S PROMISES FOR HIM

Confess your trespasses to one another,
and pray for one another, that you may be healed.
The effective, fervent prayer
of a righteous man avails much.

JAMES 5:16

He sent His word
and healed them,
and delivered them
from their destructions.

PSALM 107:20

The fear of the LORD is the beginning of knowledge, but fools despise wisdom and instruction.

PROVERBS 1:7

gifts

*Having then gifts differing according to the grace
that is given to us, let us use them.*

ROMANS 12:6

Prayer for My Son's Gifting and Purpose

LORD, I THANK YOU for the gifts and talents You have placed in my son. I pray that You would develop them in him and use them for Your glory. Show me if there is any special nurturing, training, or opportunities I should provide for him. May his gifts and talents be developed in Your way and in Your time and for Your purpose.

As he recognizes the talents and abilities You've given him, I pray that no feelings of fear or uncertainty will keep him from using them according to Your will. May he hear the call You have on his life so that he can walk forward in that purpose.

Prayer for My Son's Desire to Learn

LORD, I PRAY that (name of child) will have a deep reverence for You and Your ways. May he hide Your Word in his heart like a treasure and seek after understanding like silver or gold. Give him a good mind, a teachable spirit, and an ability to learn. Instill in him a desire to attain knowledge and skill, and may he have joy in the process.

May he never turn away from learning, but rather may he always turn to You for the knowledge he needs.

BELIEVING IN GOD'S PROMISES FOR HIM

Teach me good judgment and knowledge,
for I believe Your commandments.
Before I was afflicted I went astray,
but now I keep Your word.

PSALM 119:66-67

Every good gift and every perfect gift is from above,
and comes down from the Father of lights,
with whom there is no variation or shadow of turning.

JAMES 1:17

Blessings

SPEAK A BLESSING

As a beloved child of God, may you grow in godly wisdom
that surpasses your age and your level of learning. May you always be strong
enough to not allow others—even those older than you—to sway your convictions
of faith. Don't let their indecision, confusion, or bad choices affect
your understanding of God's path and purpose for you. May you have a
clear sense of purpose and destiny all the days of your life (1 Timothy 4:11-12).

My son, you will be presented with many false idols, fake foundations,
and faulty places of refuge. May you always resist them
and instead turn to God for protection, strength, and deliverance.
Be strong in the Lord, and do not be tempted to meet your desires your own way.
Instead, may your heart always lead you to the Lord,
who supplies all your needs (Psalm 62:1-2).

Prayer for My Son's Thoughts and Words

LORD, I PRAY that my son's heart and mind will be filled with Your Spirit and Your truth so that what comes out of his mouth will be words of life and wholeness and faith. Enable him to understand what words glorify You and what words do not.

I pray that mean words and thoughts would be so foreign to him that he is repulsed by them. Help him to hear himself so that his speech is never careless or dishonest. When he is tempted to use negative, hurtful, uncaring, or compassionless language, convict his heart and keep his words positive, kind, and filled with Your love.

BELIEVING IN GOD'S PROMISES FOR HIM

*A good man out of the good treasure of his heart
brings forth good things,
and an evil man out of the evil treasure
brings forth evil things.*

MATTHEW 12:35

Let no corrupt word proceed out of your mouth,
but what is good for necessary edification,
that it may impart grace to the hearers.

EPHESIANS 4:29

Blessed are the pure in heart,
for they shall see God.

MATTHEW 5:8

PRAYER FOR

Prayer for My Son's Passion for Holiness

LORD, MAY A desire for holiness that comes from a pure heart be reflected in all that my son does. Let it be manifested in his appearance as well. I pray that the way he dresses, acts, lives, and treats others will reflect a reverence and desire to glorify You.

If he strays from the path of holiness, bring him to repentance and work Your cleansing power in his heart and life. Give him understanding that to live in purity brings wholeness and blessing into his life, and that it is the greatest reward because it means being closer to You.

BELIEVING IN GOD'S PROMISES FOR HIM

May the Lord make you increase and abound in love
to one another and to all, just as we do to you, so that He may establish
your hearts blameless in holiness before our God and Father
at the coming of our Lord Jesus Christ with all His saints.

1 THESSALONIANS 3:12-13

Your word I have hidden in my heart, that I might not sin against You.

PSALM 119:11

Prayer for My Son's Faith in God's Word

LORD, PLANT YOUR Word in my son's heart. Let it take root in his mind and soul as he grows in Your Word daily. Grow his faith stronger each time he reads, hears, or speaks Your Word. Let verses of Scripture be engraved in his mind and on his soul so that they will be a weapon for him against any danger. Wherever there is real danger or good reason to fear, give him wisdom, protect him, and draw him close to You.

Thank You, Lord, for Your promise to deliver us from all our fears. Help him take any fears to You in prayer and seek deliverance from them so that he can walk with trust in Your power.

BELIEVING IN GOD'S PROMISES FOR HIM

Your word is a lamp to my feet and a light to my path.

PSALM 119:105

Prayer for My Son's Spirit of Joy

LORD, I PRAY that (name of child) be given the gift of joy. Let the spirit of joy rise up in his heart this day. Help him to understand that true happiness and joy are found only in You. Whenever he is overtaken by negative emotions, surround him with Your love. Teach him to say, "This is the day that the LORD has made, [I] will rejoice and be glad in it" (Psalm 118:24).

Deliver him from despair, depression, loneliness, discouragement, anger, or rejection. May these negative attitudes have no place in (name of child). Instead, let him rest in the fullness of joy that is found only in Your presence.

BELIEVING IN GOD'S PROMISES FOR HIM

If you keep My commandments, you will abide in My love,
just as I have kept My Father's commandments and abide in His love.
These things I have spoken to you, that My joy may remain in you,
and that your joy may be full.

JOHN 15:10-11

Let all those rejoice who put their trust in You;
let them ever shout for joy, because You defend them;
let those also who love Your name be joyful in You.

PSALM 5:11

PRAYER FOR A
Spirit of joy

*Having then gifts differing according to the grace
that is given to us, let us use them.*

ROMANS 12:6

Prayer for My Son's Sense of What's Right

LORD, I PRAY that You would speak clearly and strongly to my boy whenever he is tempted to do something that goes against Your best for him. Make him strong enough in You to understand the difference between right and wrong so he will always stand for what's right. Help him to resist all evil temptations and sexual immorality.

Guard him from those who give themselves over to ungodly practices or harmful and hurtful behaviors. I pray that he will understand the importance of his sexual purity so that he will honor his future marriage partner with faithfulness and innocence. May Your grace enable him to be committed to staying pure so he will honor You with his choices.

BELIEVING IN GOD'S PROMISES FOR HIM

Blessed is the man who endures temptation;
for when he has been approved,
he will receive the crown of life which the Lord
has promised to those who love Him.

JAMES 1:12

If you would earnestly seek God
and make your supplication to the Almighty,
if you were pure and upright,
surely now He would awake for you,
and prosper your rightful dwelling place.

JOB 8:5-6

Take firm hold of instruction, do not let go;
keep her, for she is your life.

PROVERBS 4:13

PRAYER FOR
direction

Prayer for My Son's Direction in Life

LORD, I PRAY that my son will respect the wisdom and direction of his parents and be willing to be taught by them. Bring perfect teachers into his life who are godly people from whom he can easily learn. Make the pathways of learning smooth and not something with which he must strain and struggle.

Give him clarity of thought, a good memory, a strong learning ability, and a sense of purpose so that he can walk with Your leading into the future for him.

BELIEVING IN GOD'S PROMISES FOR HIM

My son, hear the instruction of your father,
and do not forsake the law of your mother;
for they will be graceful ornaments on your head,
and chains about your neck.

PROVERBS 1:8-9

Prayer for My Son's Trust in God

LORD, I PRAY that You would take the faith You have planted in my son and multiply it. May the truth of Your Word be firmly established in his heart so that faith will grow daily and navigate his life. Help him to trust You at all times as he looks to You for truth, guidance, and transformation into Your likeness.

I pray he will have faith strong enough to lift him above his circumstances and instill in him the confidence of knowing that everything will work together for good for those who love You.

BELIEVING IN GOD'S PROMISES FOR HIM

Therefore, if anyone is in Christ,
he is a new creation; old things have passed away;
behold, all things have become new.

2 CORINTHIANS 5:17

*Faith is the substance
of things hoped for,
the evidence of
things not seen.*

HEBREWS 11:1

For surely there is a hereafter,
and your hope will not be cut off.
Hear, my son, and be wise;
and guide your heart in the way.

PROVERBS 23:18-19

Prayer for My Son's Life and Future

LORD, MAY A healthy fear and knowledge of You be the foundation upon which my son builds his life and future. May he turn to You for all decisions so that he doesn't make poor choices. Help him to see that all the treasures of wisdom are hidden in You and that You give of them freely when we ask for them.

As he seeks guidance from You over the years, Lord, pour it liberally upon him so that all his paths will be peace filled, his life will be blessed, and his future will be bright.

BELIEVING IN GOD'S PROMISES FOR HIM

The mercy of the LORD is from everlasting to everlasting on those who fear Him, and His righteousness to children's children, to such as keep His covenant, and to those who remember His commandments to do them.

PSALM 103:17-18

SPEAK A BLESSING

Dear Son, I want nothing more than for you to

always keep God's Word, live in His truth,

and fulfill His purpose for your life.

May you live in all the goodness that God has for you.

May you be perfected by His love and life flowing through you.

May you learn to not rely on your own strength

so that you grow weary,

but rather to lean on the Lord's strength

so that you are renewed in His presence.

May you always trust His working in your life (1 John 2:5).

Blessings

Storms will come and go in your life.

There will be many worldly and unstable lifelines thrown in your direction.

But if you refuse to grasp for them, and instead hold fast to the covenant, testimonies, and promises of the Lord, you will see Him either bring you through the storm or lift you above it to a place of rest and comfort.

You will see Him calm the storms, soothe your soul, and draw you to a place of safety.

That's because all the paths of the Lord are mercy and truth (Psalm 25:10).

Blessed be One

Blessed be the God and Father of our Lord Jesus Christ,

who has blessed us with every spiritual blessing

in the heavenly places in Christ,

just as He chose us in Him before the foundation of the world,

that we should be holy and without blame before Him in love,

having predestined us to adoption as sons

by Jesus Christ to Himself, according to the good pleasure

of His will, to the praise of the glory of His grace,

by which He has made us accepted in the Beloved.

EPHESIANS 1:3-6